AF270465

THE BEST OF WORLD SOCCER

THE BEST MEN'S PLAYERS OF WORLD SOCCER

BY LUKE HANLON

SportsZone

An Imprint of Abdo Publishing
abdobooks.com

abdobooks.com

Published by Abdo Publishing, a division of ABDO, PO Box 398166, Minneapolis, Minnesota 55439. Copyright © 2024 by Abdo Consulting Group, Inc. International copyrights reserved in all countries. No part of this book may be reproduced in any form without written permission from the publisher. SportsZone™ is a trademark and logo of Abdo Publishing.

Printed in China.
102023
012024

Editor: Charlie Beattie
Series Designers: Karli Kruse and Joshua Olson

Library of Congress Control Number: 2023939435

Publisher's Cataloging-in-Publication Data

Names: Hanlon, Luke, author.
Title: The best men's players of world soccer / by Luke Hanlon
Description: Minneapolis, Minnesota: Abdo Publishing, 2024 | Series: The best of world soccer | Includes online resources and index.
Identifiers: ISBN 9781098292270 (lib. bdg.) | ISBN 9798384910213 (ebook)
Subjects: LCSH: Soccer--Juvenile literature. | Professional sports--Juvenile literature. | Soccer players--Juvenile literature. | World Cup (Soccer)--Juvenile literature. | Soccer--Records--Juvenile literature.
Classification: DDC 796.334--dc23

TABLE OF CONTENTS

CHAPTER 1

EARLY STARS

The first World Cup tournament in 1930 featured 13 men's teams. Italy was not one of them. But four years later the European nation hosted the tournament. Giuseppe Meazza played center forward for Italy. Though he lacked in size, Meazza made up for it with skilled footwork and an accurate

shot. *Il Balilla*, or "the Little Boy," scored two goals in five games despite battling an injury during the tournament. After Italy beat Czechoslovakia 2–1 in the final, Meazza was named the tournament's best player.

Four years later, Meazza captained Italy to a second straight World Cup title. When he wasn't playing for the national team, Meazza starred for Inter Milan, which was establishing itself as one of the country's best clubs. In 1980 the stadium Inter shares with rival AC Milan was renamed after Meazza.

MASTERS OF MADRID

For years, men's European club teams played only against other clubs from their country. That changed in 1955–56 with the creation of the European Cup. The tournament, which was renamed the Champions League in 1992–93, features the best teams from each European country. One club dominated its early years. Led by Alfredo Di Stéfano, Real Madrid won the first three European Cup titles. A natural scorer as a forward, Di Stéfano was also known for his defensive effort and versatility. And Di Stéfano saved his best for big matches. He scored in each of those three finals.

Real Madrid gave Di Stéfano a lethal strike partner in 1958. Ferenc Puskás was recognized as the game's best goal scorer of

the 1950s. He had already helped make his native Hungary an international force. Puskás scored most of his 83 international goals with his lethal left foot. Now with Puskás lining up alongside Di Stéfano, Real Madrid was almost impossible to stop. The club ran its European Cup streak to five straight. The 1960 final might have been the finest hour for both Di Stéfano and Puskás. Real Madrid smashed German side Eintracht Frankfurt 7–3. Di Stéfano scored three goals, and Puskás added the other four.

Alfredo Di Stéfano, *bottom row, center,* and Ferenc Puskás, *bottom row, second from right,* led a powerful Real Madrid team in the late 1950s and early 1960s.

THE BEAUTIFUL GAME

While Real Madrid dominated European club soccer in the late 1950s and early 1960s, Brazil was emerging as the newest international power. The South American country was stacked with talent. However, no player stood out more than Pelé. Soccer elevated from a sport to an art when Pelé graced the field. While it is disputed who first called soccer "the beautiful game," it was Pelé who popularized the term. He dazzled fans with his dribbling flair. And he personified Brazil's fast-paced style.

At only 17, Pelé was the youngest player at the 1958 World Cup. He scored a hat trick in the semifinals against France.

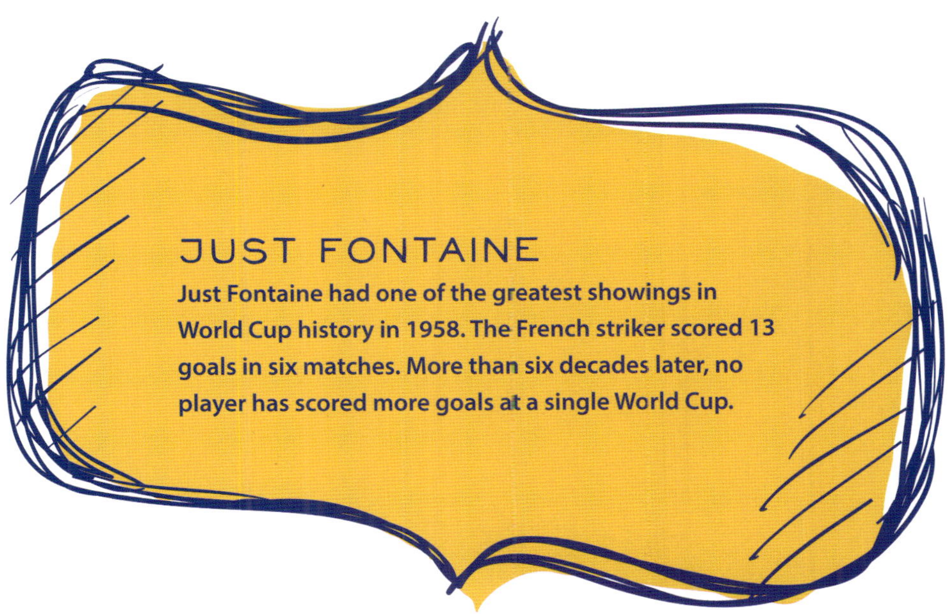

JUST FONTAINE

Just Fontaine had one of the greatest showings in World Cup history in 1958. The French striker scored 13 goals in six matches. More than six decades later, no player has scored more goals at a single World Cup.

Just four minutes into the final, however, Brazil fell behind host Sweden 1–0. It was time for leadership, and that came from one of Brazil's oldest players. Midfielder Didi was 29 in 1958. After Sweden's goal, he slowly walked to the center circle for the kickoff. When one of his teammates told Didi to hurry up, the captain told him to relax. "We're better than them. We'll score goals aplenty," he said.

Didi was right. Brazil tied the game less than five minutes later. The South American side went on to win 5–2, with Pelé scoring twice. Though the youngster went home having announced himself as a star, it was Didi who was named the tournament's best player. However, Pelé would go on to win additional World Cup titles in 1962 and 1970. Popular with fans around the world, Pelé also helped grow the sport in the United States when he ended his playing career with the New York Cosmos.

Didi played in three World Cups for Brazil, winning twice.

Lev Yashin, *left,* smothers the ball before West Germany's Uwe Seeler can get to it during a 1966 World Cup game.

BLACK SPIDER

The Soviet Union was one of the teams Brazil had to beat at the 1958 World Cup. Brazil had the better team, but the Soviets had Lev Yashin. The goalkeeper frustrated the Brazilian attack. While Brazil ended up beating the Soviets 2–0, many journalists left the game praising Yashin as the best goalkeeper in the world.

Yashin's reflexes and dark jersey earned him the nickname "Black Spider." And while his shot stopping was elite, it was his style of play that stood out. At the time, most goalkeepers never moved far from the net. Yashin often rushed far out of

Bobby Charlton, *holding trophy,* and Bobby Moore, *to Charlton's right,* celebrate after England's win in the 1966 World Cup final.

his penalty area to cut off angles of attackers. He also was one of the first keepers to bark out orders to his teammates during a match. Yashin's skills and trailblazing style earned him the 1963 Ballon d'Or, which is considered the sport's most

prestigious individual award. Sixty years later, he was still the
only goalkeeper to have won it.

THE TWO BOBBYS

Many defenders tried to slow Pelé over the years, often
unsuccessfully. The Brazilian superstar called Bobby Moore
the best defender he ever played against. Moore captained
England to the World Cup title on home soil in 1966. England
manager Alf Ramsey thought so highly of his captain's
leadership that he said he could trust his life to Moore.

Moore was the rock of England's defense. Leading its attack
was Bobby Charlton. The attacking midfielder possessed
a thundering shot and used it often to score from long
range. Charlton was a star at one of England's biggest clubs,
Manchester United. He was named the best player at the
1966 World Cup. He also won that year's Ballon d'Or award.
Charlton's shining moment came in the World Cup semifinals
against Portugal. He scored both of England's goals in a
2–1 win.

BACK ON TOP

In 1970 Brazil put together what many experts call the greatest
national team ever. At 29 Pelé was still the world's best player.
But he had plenty of help. Right back Carlos Alberto was

Brazil's leader. Midfielder Gerson was an excellent playmaker, while winger Rivellino was one of the best dribblers of his era. His signature move was known as both the "Elastico" and the "Flip Flap." It was a quick tap of the ball one way, before pulling it back the other direction. Defenders everywhere struggled to stop it.

The team's striker was Jairzinho. He used his powerful shots to score in every game of the 1970 World Cup in Mexico. Brazil rolled to the title by scoring 19 goals in six matches. Fans today still marvel at the team's incredible collection of talent and style.

Pelé scored 77 times in 92 career matches for Brazil.

CHAPTER 2

ADVANCING THE GAME

West Germany lost in the semifinals of the 1970 World Cup. But Gerd Müller still managed to pile up 10 goals at the tournament in Mexico. Goal scoring was nothing new to the striker. He had led his country's top league, the Bundesliga, in goals scored for two straight years.

Müller played club soccer for Bayern Munich. And he wasn't the only West German star on the club. Franz Beckenbauer began his career as a midfielder. He played for West Germany's losing team in the 1966 World Cup final. By the early 1970s he had moved back to defense. At the time, most defenders weren't asked to do too much. They usually just tried to win the ball back and get rid of it quickly. *Der Kaiser*, or "the Emperor," was different. He brought the dribbling skills he learned from his midfield years, and he revolutionized defense. When his teams were on attack, Beckenbauer rushed up to join the offense. He is often credited with creating a new position, which is now called the sweeper.

By 1972 Müller and Beckenbauer were at the top of their games. In that year's European Championship, Müller scored a tournament-leading five goals. That included two goals in each of the semifinal and final to help West Germany win the tournament for the first time. Beckenbauer was the captain of the squad. He kept that role for the 1974 World Cup, which West Germany hosted. The home team cruised to the final by allowing only three goals in its first six matches. Facing the Netherlands in the final, West Germany met another one of the game's transcendent players.

TOTAL STAR

In the first minute of the 1974 World Cup final, a skinny midfielder named Johan Cruyff danced through the West German defense. After beating several players, he was chopped down in the penalty area. The referee awarded the Netherlands a penalty, and the team scored to go up 1–0.

It was no surprise that Cruyff helped create a goal for the Netherlands. He had been the heartbeat of the team for years. The Dutch played a revolutionary style called "Total Football"

Franz Beckenbauer makes a move up the field while playing for German club Bayern Munich.

that had players moving all over the field and frequently changing positions. The team's players had to be versatile, and no one was better than Cruyff. The "Flying Dutchman" was on his way to a third Ballon d'Or in 1974. His dribbling skills were unmatched. Cruyff's signature move was faking a shot or pass and then hooking the ball back behind his other leg to change direction. It became known as the "Cruyff Turn."

Johan Cruyff played only 48 games for the Netherlands but scored 33 times.

However, Beckenbauer and the West German defense managed to contain Cruyff and the feared Dutch attack for the rest of the 1974 final. West Germany tied the game on a first-half penalty. Just before halftime, Müller fired a low shot into the corner. It was his record 14th career World Cup goal as West Germany held on to win 2–1.

THE GOLDEN BOY

In the summer of 1984, a hotshot young star arrived in Serie A, Italy's top league. The southern team Napoli signed attacking midfielder Diego Maradona. He had been labeled a prodigy before he even turned 10 in his native Argentina. In a nation suffering from terrible economic problems, *El Pibe de Oro*, "the Golden Boy," was seen as a savior both on and off the field.

Maradona's dribbling skills and quick moves with the ball were unlike anything onlookers had yet seen. And despite standing just 5 feet, 5 inches tall, Maradona could play a physical style. He used his low center of gravity and strong, thick legs to avoid tackles or simply run through them. At the 1986 World Cup in Mexico, defenders fouled him constantly, but nothing slowed him down.

His most legendary match came against England in the tournament's quarterfinal round. Early in the second half, Maradona went after a looping cross in the England

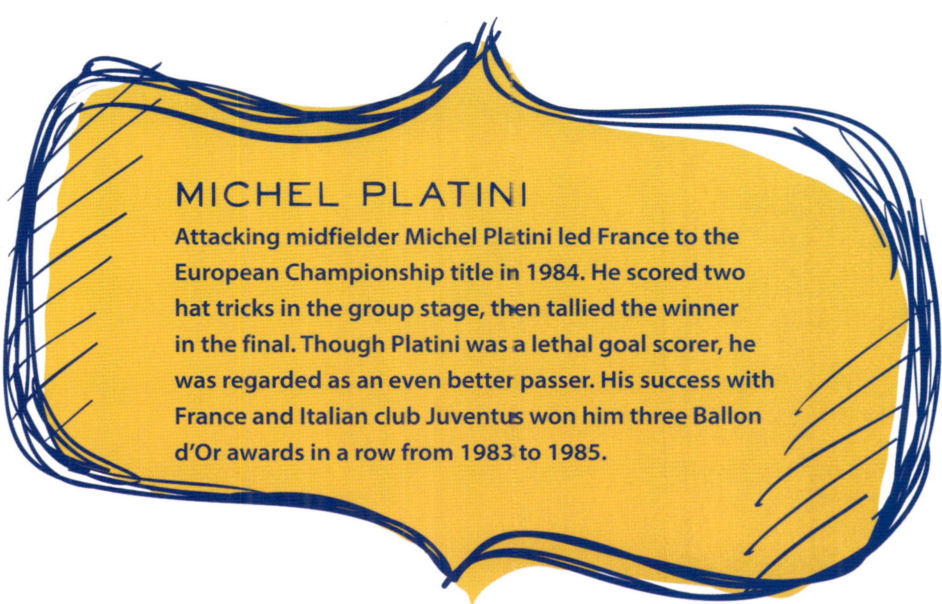

penalty area. He appeared to outjump 6-foot English keeper Peter Shilton for the ball and head it into the net. Replays showed that Maradona had actually hidden his fist near his head. He used it to punch the ball into the net. The referees didn't spot it, so the goal stood. After the match, Maradona was quoted as saying the goal was scored "a little bit with the head of Diego and a little with the hand of God." The "Hand of God" goal remains one of the most famous moments in soccer history.

While his first goal in the match was technically illegal, Maradona's second was pure magic. He gained possession of the ball in his own half and dribbled nearly 70 yards through a host of English defenders before scoring the winning goal in a 2–1 victory. That run became known as the "Goal of the Century."

Maradona scored two more goals in the semifinals against Belgium. Then in the final, he set up the winner in a 3–2 victory over West Germany. The Golden Ball award had

Maradona celebrates with Napoli fans after leading the club to the Serie A title in 1987.

been introduced at the 1982 World Cup as an honor to the tournament's best player. Maradona won the award in 1986.

Maradona enhanced his legend even more after returning to Napoli. For years Serie A was dominated by teams in northern Italy. That region had more money than the southern region, where Napoli plays. Maradona had grown up in a town without running water. His hardscrabble background made him a natural hero for the people of Naples, a city that long had issues with organized crime and poverty. He lifted Napoli to its first Serie A title in 1987. The club won the league title again in 1990. That turned Maradona into a folk hero not just in his home country, but also in his adopted city of Naples.

ROCKS OF ITALY

During Maradona's reign at Napoli, the Italian league was best known for its defenders. A pair of Italians exemplified that. Franco Baresi first played for AC Milan in the 1977–78 season. Paolo Maldini joined him in 1984–85. Each played for more than 20 seasons with the famous club.

Baresi was small for a defender. And he didn't talk much. However, he led by example with perfectly timed tackles and a strong sense of where to be to cut off attacks. His skill on the ball was often compared to Beckenbauer's, so much so that fans called Baresi "Kaiser Franz."

Though Maldini had stints at fullback, he mainly played as a center back. Either way, he could adapt to his teammates' strengths and play where the team needed him. In his 25-year career, Maldini set a Serie A record with 647 appearances. He was also known for his clean play. Maldini was red carded only three times in his career. He won seven

<< **Franco Baresi was AC Milan's captain for 15 years before retiring in 1997.**

Paolo Maldini took over as AC Milan's captain after Baresi retired.

CHAPTER 3

A NEW CENTURY

league titles, and Baresi won six. The two also teamed up to win the European Cup three times.

As Brazil and France walked out to kick off the 1998 World Cup final in Saint-Denis, France, fans watching had a right to be starstruck. Both sides were loaded with talent. Brazil had two star fullbacks with Cafú on the right and Roberto Carlos on the left. Up front, 21-year-old striker Ronaldo was just beginning a record-setting career.

Brazil was the defending champion, but any chance of repeating was undone by one man. France midfielder Zinédine Zidane rose from a tough upbringing in the southern city of Marseille. At age 26, he was the star of the French national team. Opponents marveled at Zidane's skills and playmaking

FREE-KICK SPECIALISTS

Roberto Carlos scored 49 free-kick goals in his career. But he was just one free-kick specialist playing in the 1990s and 2000s. Italian Andrea Pirlo was a master of accurate shots. In England David Beckham's swerving shots inspired a movie called *Bend It Like Beckham*. They also helped make him one of the most famous players of his generation.

Zidane joined Real Madrid in 2001. One of his teammates
was Roberto Carlos. And Zidane showed that his knack for big
goals extended to club soccer as well. Real Madrid was tied 1–1
with German team Bayer Leverkusen late in the first half of the
2002 Champions League final. Roberto Carlos sent a looping
cross to Zidane at the edge of the penalty area. Zidane swung
his left leg and connected with the ball just below shoulder
height. Despite the awkward angle, he struck the shot sweetly
into the net. One of the most famous goals in Champions
League history won the title for Real Madrid.

TALENT WINS

Brazil entered the 2002 World Cup loaded with superstars. Cafú
was still a key member of the team. Now 25, Ronaldo was in his
prime. Midfielder Rivaldo had won the Ballon d'Or in 1999.

The team also had a new 22-year-old trickster playing in
the midfield. Ronaldinho believed soccer was supposed to
be entertaining, so he set out to make the game exciting. His
clever footwork frustrated defenders but thrilled crowds. The
midfielder used his dazzling skills to score sensational goals.

Ronaldo, *left,* and Ronaldinho celebrate one of Ronaldo's eight goals at the 2002 World Cup.

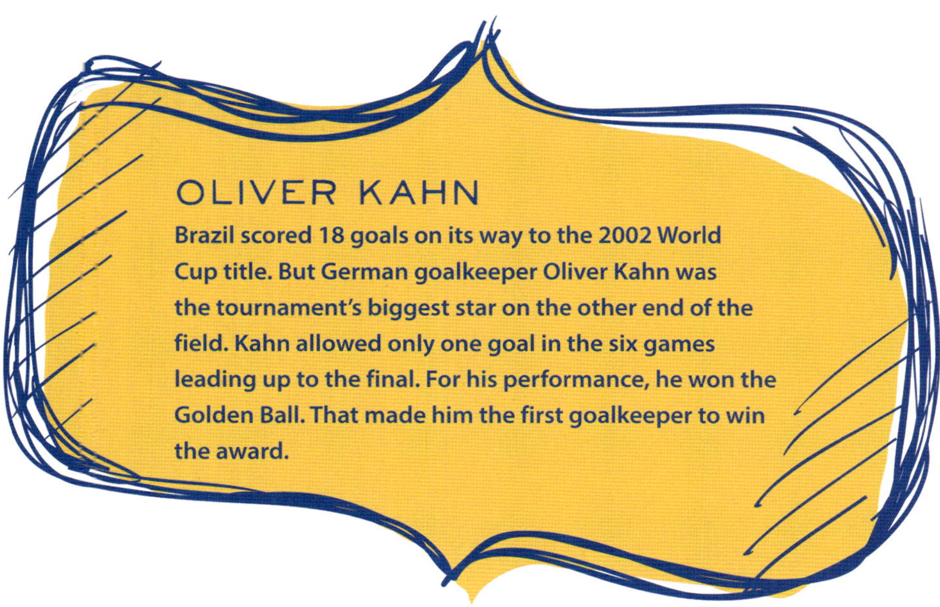

Once, while playing for Barcelona, Ronaldinho scored twice on the road against archrival Real Madrid. After the second goal, an impressive long solo run, the Madrid fans gave him a standing ovation.

After Ronaldinho sank England in the 2002 quarterfinals with a goal on a long free kick, Ronaldo took over for the rest of the tournament. He scored twice in the final to beat Germany and win Brazil's record fifth title. The goals were Ronaldo's seventh and eighth of the tournament.

Gianluigi Buffon was on Italy's roster for five consecutive World Cups from 1998 to 2014.

GIGI

At 33 years old, Zidane was back atop his game at the 2006 World Cup. He once again guided France back to the final. It was the retiring star's final game. And after France earned a penalty early in the match, Zidane had the chance to go out as a hero.

Zidane stepped up to the spot to face one of the sport's best goalkeepers. At 6 feet, 4 inches tall with long arms, Italy's 28-year-old Gianluigi Buffon looked like he filled up the entire net. "Gigi" often played like it as well. The lanky keeper was known as an excellent shot stopper, especially in big matches.

This time Zidane reached deep into his bag of tricks. He took a hard run up to the ball, then lightly chipped it toward the net. Buffon went the wrong way, and the soft shot ricocheted down off the crossbar before settling into the goal.

The brave shot once again showed Zidane thrived under pressure. However, his temper took over later in the match. With the teams tied in extra time, Italian defender Marco Materazzi taunted Zidane. Suddenly Zidane wheeled around and headbutted the defender squarely in the chest. The superstar was immediately given a red card. It was an unlikely end to one of the sport's great careers.

Meanwhile, Zidane's early penalty was just the second goal Buffon had allowed all tournament. For the rest of the game,

Iker Casillas, *right,* stops a shot from the Netherlands' Arjen Robben with his foot during the 2010 World Cup final.

his saves kept France off the board. Italy went on to win in a penalty shootout. It was a crowning moment for Buffon, but his career was far from over. He returned to his club team, Juventus, and helped it win eight Serie A titles from 2012 to 2020. In 2020 Buffon broke Paolo Maldini's record for the most Serie A appearances.

TIKI–TAKA

Spain has always had skilled players, and its top professional league, La Liga, is one of the best in the world. But entering the

Andrés Iniesta scores the winning goal for Spain in the 2010 World Cup final.

2000s the country had never won a World Cup. There was new optimism, however, as a crop of talented young players were all emerging at once.

Most of the team's stars played for the nation's two biggest clubs. Calm, cat-quick goalkeeper Iker Casillas played for

Real Madrid. Hard-nosed defender Sergio Ramos played with him there.

Another rugged defender, Carles Puyol, starred for Barcelona. A smaller center back at 5 feet, 10 inches, Puyol made up for it with his physicality. His ong, curly hair swirled as he flew into tackles. And he made a habit out of putting his body at risk to block hard shots.

In midfield, Barcelona had both Xavi and Andrés Iniesta. The club played a brand of soccer known as "tiki-taka." It required patience and precise passing. Both Xavi and Iniesta were masters of keeping possession. They could both dribble in tight areas without losing the ball. And each had the talent to play a perfect pass to an open striker when the chance arose.

That group of club rivals led Spain to European Championship success in 2008. Two years later, Spain was battling in a scoreless World Cup final against the Netherlands. Early in the second half, Dutch striker Arjen Robben broke through the Spanish defense. He tried a low shot to Casillas's right. The goalkeeper quickly stuck out a leg and managed to tip it around the post.

That kept the game scoreless into extra time. In the final minutes, Iniesta found space in the box. He settled a hard pass and let the ball bounce in front of him. Iniesta then smashed home the winning goal.

CHAPTER 4

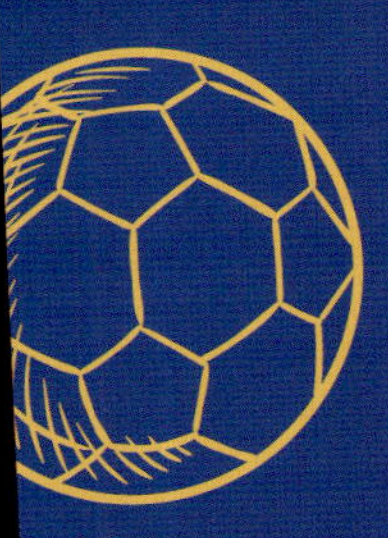

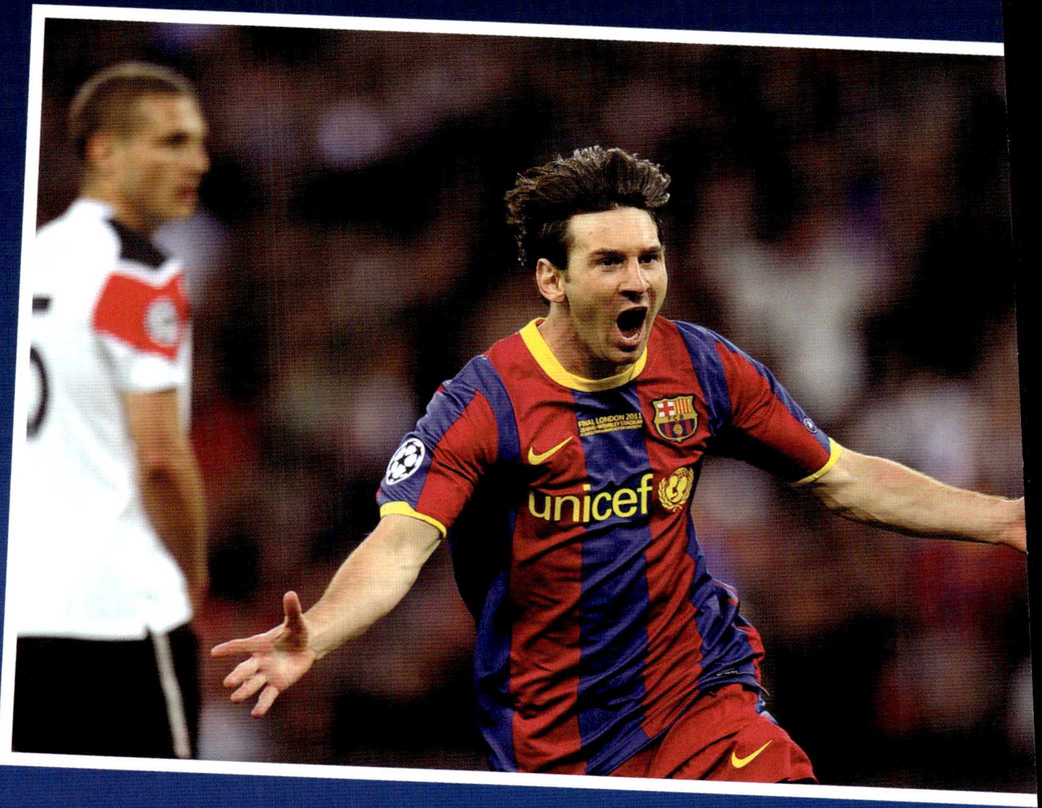

MODERN LEGENDS

Two years later, Spain's superstars captured a third straight major international title. Xavi put on a passing master class in the European Championship game against Italy. His two assists

Lionel Messi debuted for Barcelona in 2005 at age 17. Within three years, he was one of the world's most feared goal scorers. The only thing Messi did not have was size. He needed daily hormone injections throughout childhood for the forward grow to his full height of 5 feet, 7 inches. But his quick feet and speed made up for his height deficiency. Messi could dribble through the smallest opening. And his pinpoint left-footed shots humbled goalkeepers all over the world.

From an early age, Messi was seen in his native Argentina as the second coming of Diego Maradona. Like Maradona he led his European club to success. With Messi piling up goals, Barcelona won 10 La Liga and four European titles. One of his most famous moments came in the 2012 Champions League round of 16 against German club Bayer Leverkusen. Messi scored five times to help Barcelona advance.

Barcelona's rival, Real Madrid, had its own superstar scorer. Portuguese striker Cristiano Ronaldo first made his name for Manchester United in England. But after Ronaldo joined Real Madrid in 2009, the two superstars went head to head at least twice every season. The Spanish term for the Real Madrid/ Barcelona rivalry is *El Clásico*, meaning "the Classic." Ronaldo and Messi made sure they lived up to the billing. Ronaldo's skills included a powerful running stride and an exceptionally

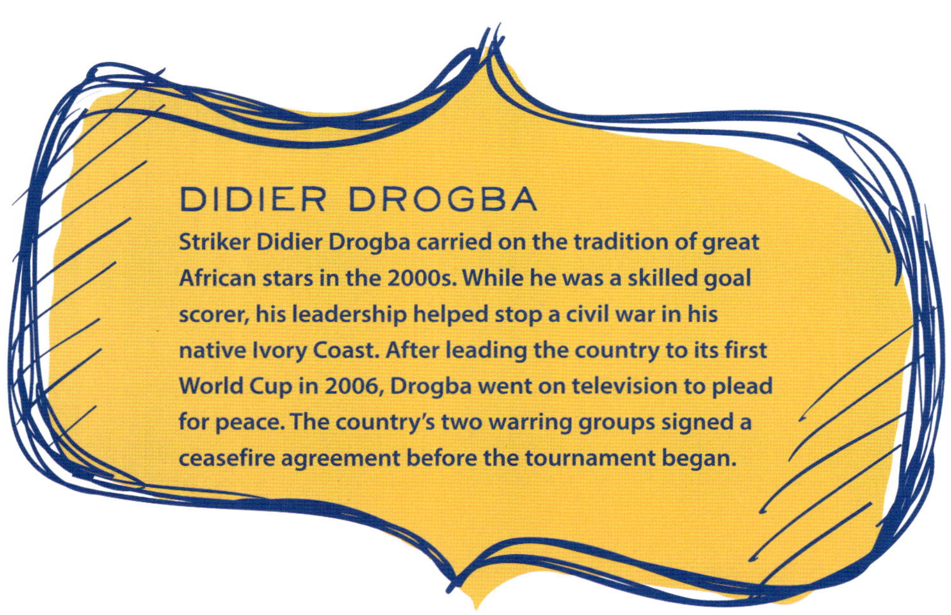

HALA MADRID

Real Madrid has always had superstars, and in the 2000s, defender Sergio Ramos was a physical force. He used his punishing tackling to put opposing forwards off their game. This aggressive style sometimes led Ramos over the edge. He was red carded 26 times while playing for Real Madrid. But he

Sergio Ramos, *left*, and Luka Modrić played together for nine seasons at Real Madrid.

also helped the club win five La Liga titles and four Champions League crowns. In addition, Ramos was a key player for Spain's two European Championship winners in 2008 and 2012 and the nation's only World Cup title in 2010.

He also had a knack for big goals. In the 2014 Champions League final, Ramos scored a header with just seconds left in regulation to tie crosstown rival Atletico Madrid 1–1. Real went on to win 4–1 in extra time.

Neymar scored his 77th goal for Brazil during the 2022 World Cup. That tied him with Pelé for the most goals scored in Brazil's history.

Running the midfield for Real Madrid during the decade was Croatian Luka Modrić. The 5-foot-8-inch midfielder developed into one of the most creative passers the world had ever seen. He joined Madrid before the 2012–13 season. A year later the club won its first Champions League title in 12 years.

In Madrid, Modrić could sometimes be overlooked on a squad filled with superstars. That wasn't the case for Croatia. In 2018 he was the driving force as the underdog nation made a run to the World Cup final. Croatia came up just short against a powerful French team, but Modrić won the Golden Ball award. He was also the Ballon d'Or winner that year.

BRAZILIAN PRODIGY

Brazilian fans started hyping up Neymar to be the nation's next big star when he was a teenager. It didn't take long for him to prove those fans right. The forward started playing for Brazil's national team when he was 18. Neymar used jaw-dropping dribbling skills to create space for himself to score or to set up teammates. But his first few international tournaments ended in disappointment. Brazil lost in the gold-medal game at the 2012 Olympics. Then Neymar suffered an injury during the 2014 World Cup. He had to watch his team lose 7–1 to Germany in the semifinals.

Manuel Neuer (1) holds up the World Cup trophy after Germany's extra-time win over Argentina in the 2014 final.

Brazil hosted the Olympics in 2016. Despite the country's rich history in the World Cup, it had never won an Olympic gold medal. Now 24, Neymar was Brazil's captain in the tournament and led the hosts to the gold-medal game against Germany. He opened the scoring with a stunning free-kick goal. The game eventually went to a penalty shootout with the score tied 1–1. After nine shooters, the teams were tied at 4–4. Neymar stepped to the spot with a chance to secure the gold medal. His shot rippled the top of the net to crown Brazil Olympic champions for the first time.

THE SWEEPER KEEPER

Like Lev Yashin in the 1950s and 1960s, Germany's Manuel Neuer revolutionized goalkeeping in the 2000s. He began to roam far outside his penalty area to intercept long balls before oncoming forwards could get to them. Neuer was also skilled enough with his feet that his defenders could comfortably pass back to him. He even recorded seven career assists on accurate long balls to strikers. Soon other goaltenders began honing these skills to become known as "sweeper keepers."

Despite the improvement of others, Neuer remained one of the sport's best goaltenders for two decades after his 2003 debut. He joined German giant Bayern Munich in 2011. In 2023

he helped Bayern win its 11th straight Bundesliga title. He also
led his country to World Cup glory in 2014.

Kylian Mbappé's eight goals were the most of any player at the 2022 World Cup.

BRIGHT FUTURE

For all their club success, Ronaldo and Messi were not as lucky on the world stage. Ronaldo finally led Portugal to a win at the European Championship in 2016. Messi had to wait even longer.

His Argentina team fell in the final at the 2014 World Cup. Then a new, young superstar overshadowed him in the round of 16 at the 2018 tournament. With Argentina and France tied 2–2 in the 64th minute, 19-year-old French forward Kylian Mbappé used his blazing speed to score twice in four minutes. France held on for a 4–3 win. Just 15 days later, Mbappé scored France's fourth goal in a 4–2 win over Modrić's Croatia in the

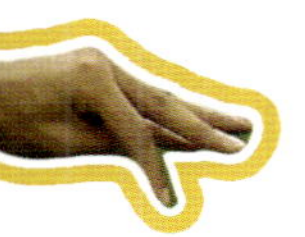

ZLATAN IBRAHIMOVIĆ

Perhaps no one was more confident than Swedish striker Zlatan Ibrahimović. He often compared himself to lions, kings, and gods. Ibrahimović backed up the talk with incredible goals. One of his most famous came in a 2012 match against England. After spotting the goalkeeper too far out, Ibrahimović scored on a bicycle kick from 30 yards away.

final. With that Mbappé became the first teenager to score in a World Cup final since Pelé in 1958.

Four years later, Messi and Mbappé met again at the 2022 World Cup in Qatar. This time it came in the final. Messi scored early as Argentina got off to a 2–0 start. But when it looked like France was out of it, Mbappé scored twice in the final 10 minutes to send the match to extra time. In extra time, Messi scored again to put Argentina up 3–2, only for Mbappé to tie the match again with a late penalty kick. That goal made him the first player to score a hat trick in a men's World Cup final since England's Geoff Hurst in 1966.

By then Messi had already won his first major championship with Argentina. The team won the Copa América to become South American champions in 2021. However, no victory cements a player's legacy like the World Cup. After Argentina outlasted France in a shootout, Messi was finally a World Cup champion.

Mbappé, meanwhile, was still in the early stages of his career. He had already played in two World Cup finals. With Messi nearing the end of his career, Mbappé had shown he was ready to be the sport's next great superstar.

The Frenchman was hardly alone as a star of the next generation. There were also many young talents ready to make their mark alongside Mbappé. Norway's 6-foot-4-inch

Erling Haaland (9) broke the English Premier League record for goals in a season by scoring 36 in 2022–23, his first season with Manchester City.

GLOSSARY

CAPTAIN
A team's leader on the field.

CLUB
The team a player competes with outside of his or her national team.

CROSS
A pass delivered from the side of the field toward the middle.

EXTRA TIME
Two 15-minute periods added to a tournament game if the score is tied at the end of regulation.

FREE KICK
An unguarded kick awarded to a team after an opponent's foul.

HAT TRICK
Three or more goals by the same player in one game.

PENALTY AREA
The box in front of the goal where a player is granted a penalty kick if he or she is fouled.

POVERTY
The state of being extremely poor.

PRODIGY
A young player who has a great natural ability for a sport.

RED CARD
A punishment given to a player, usually for violent conduct or dangerous play, that ejects that player from the rest of the game.

SHOOTOUT
A series of penalty kicks held after extra time to decide who wins a game.

VERSATILE
Able to perform many different roles or functions.

MORE INFORMATION

BOOKS

Donnelly, Patrick. *The Best Managers of World Soccer.* Minneapolis, MN: Abdo Publishing, 2024.

Hewson, Anthony K. *GOATs of Soccer.* Minneapolis, MN: Abdo Publishing, 2022.

McDougall, Chrös. *The Best Women's Players of World Soccer.* Minneapolis, MN: Abdo Publishing, 2024.

ONLINE RESOURCES

To learn more about men's soccer, please visit **abdobooklinks.com** or scan this QR code. These links are routinely monitored and updated to provide the most current information available.

INDEX

ABOUT THE AUTHOR

Luke Hanlon is a sportswriter and editor based in Minneapolis, Minnesota.